HOUSEHOLDER BOOKS

WHO IS GOD TO YOU?

THE ABCS OF WHO GOD IS

WRITTEN BY
OYIN ISAAC

ART BY
TOLUWANIMI BABARINDE

Illustrations and Book Design by Toluwanimi Babarinde

Send inquiries to hello@householderpublishing.com

Printed in Canada

Paperback ISBN: 978-10-68825-20-0

Hardcover ISBN: 979-88-69336-61-3

This book is owned by

A
1 Corinthians 15:28
He is my All in All.

B
Acts 17:28
He is my Breath and my Being.

2 Corinthians 1:3-4, Psalms 23
C
He is my Comforter and my Caregiver.

D
Psalms 18:1-6
He is my Deliverer and my Defender.

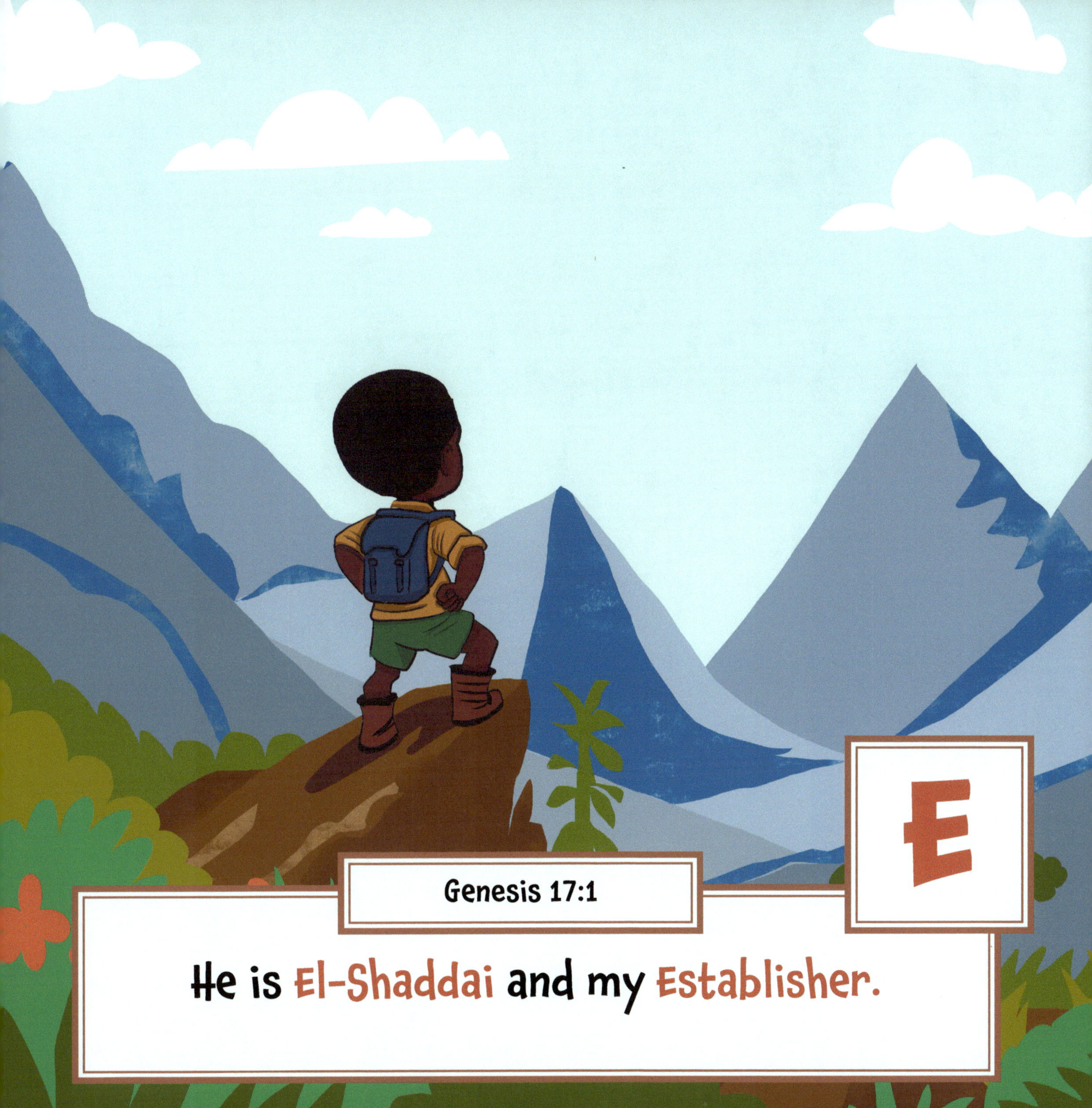
Genesis 17:1
E
He is El-Shaddai and my Establisher.

F
Isaiah 64:8
He is my Father.

Psalms 63:1
He is my God.
G

H
Psalms 121:1-2
He is my Helper.

Romans 8:16
He is my Identity.
1

J

Genesis 22:14, Exodus 6:2-3

He is my Jehovah.

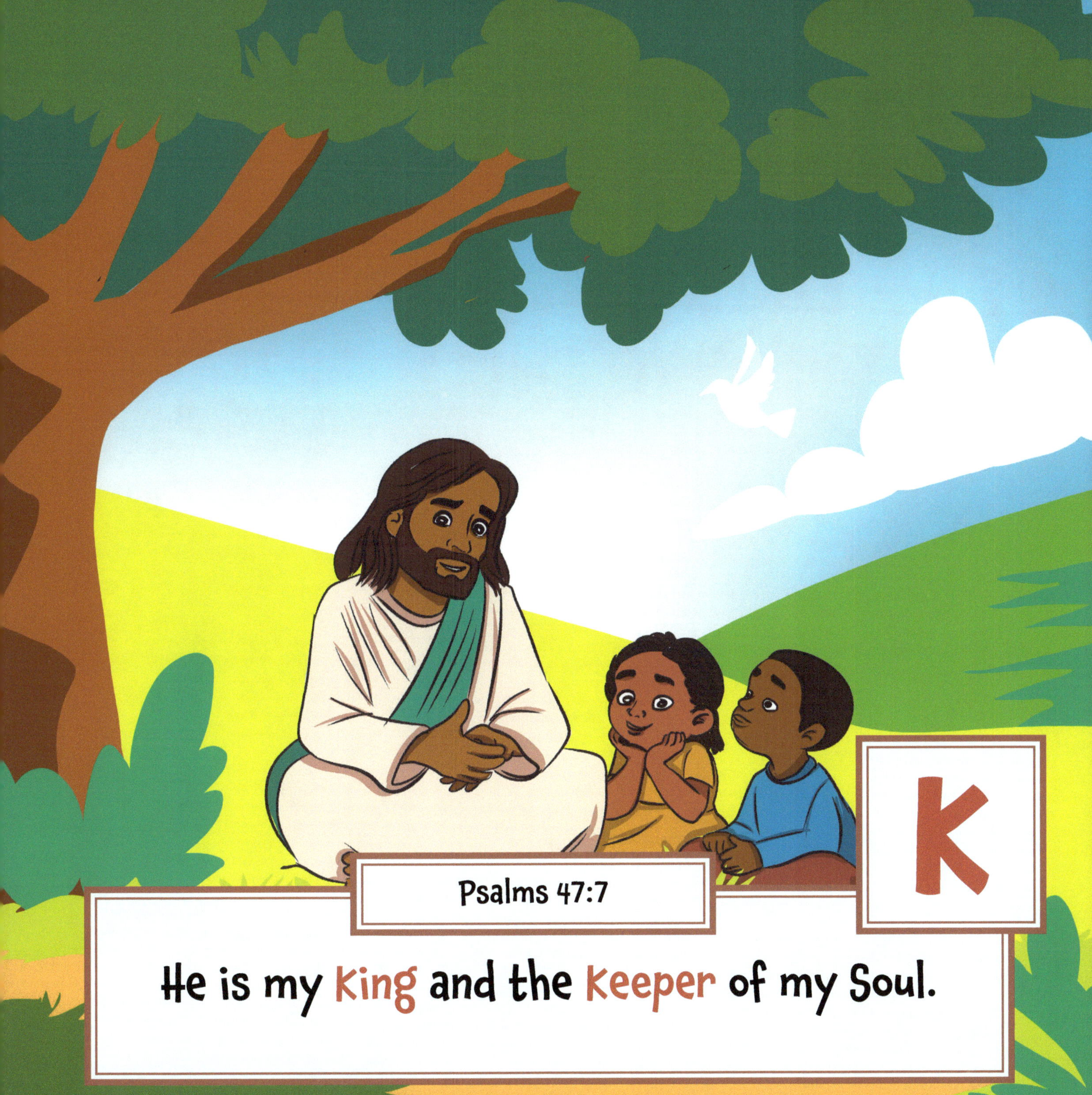
Psalms 47:7
K
He is my King and the Keeper of my Soul.

L
John 15:13
He is the Lover of my Soul.

Isaiah 54:5
M
He is my Maker.

Proverbs 3:5-6

He is my Number-One Priority.

He is my Omnipotent God.

P
Philippians 4:19, Genesis 22:14
He is my Provider.

Psalms 18:30, 2 Samuel 22:31,
Deuteronomy 32:4

Q

He is my Quintessential Father.

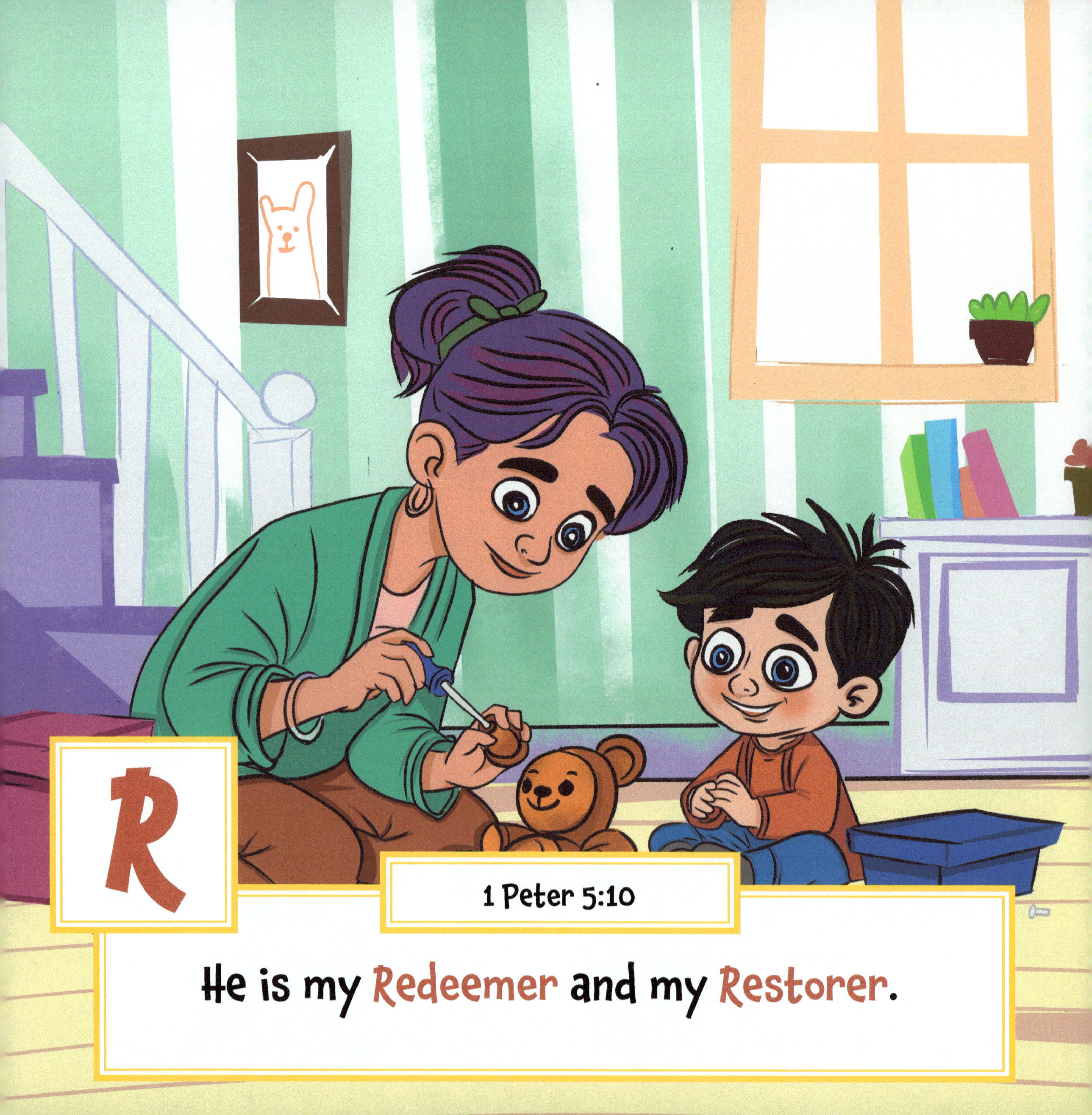
R
1 Peter 5:10
He is my Redeemer and my Restorer.

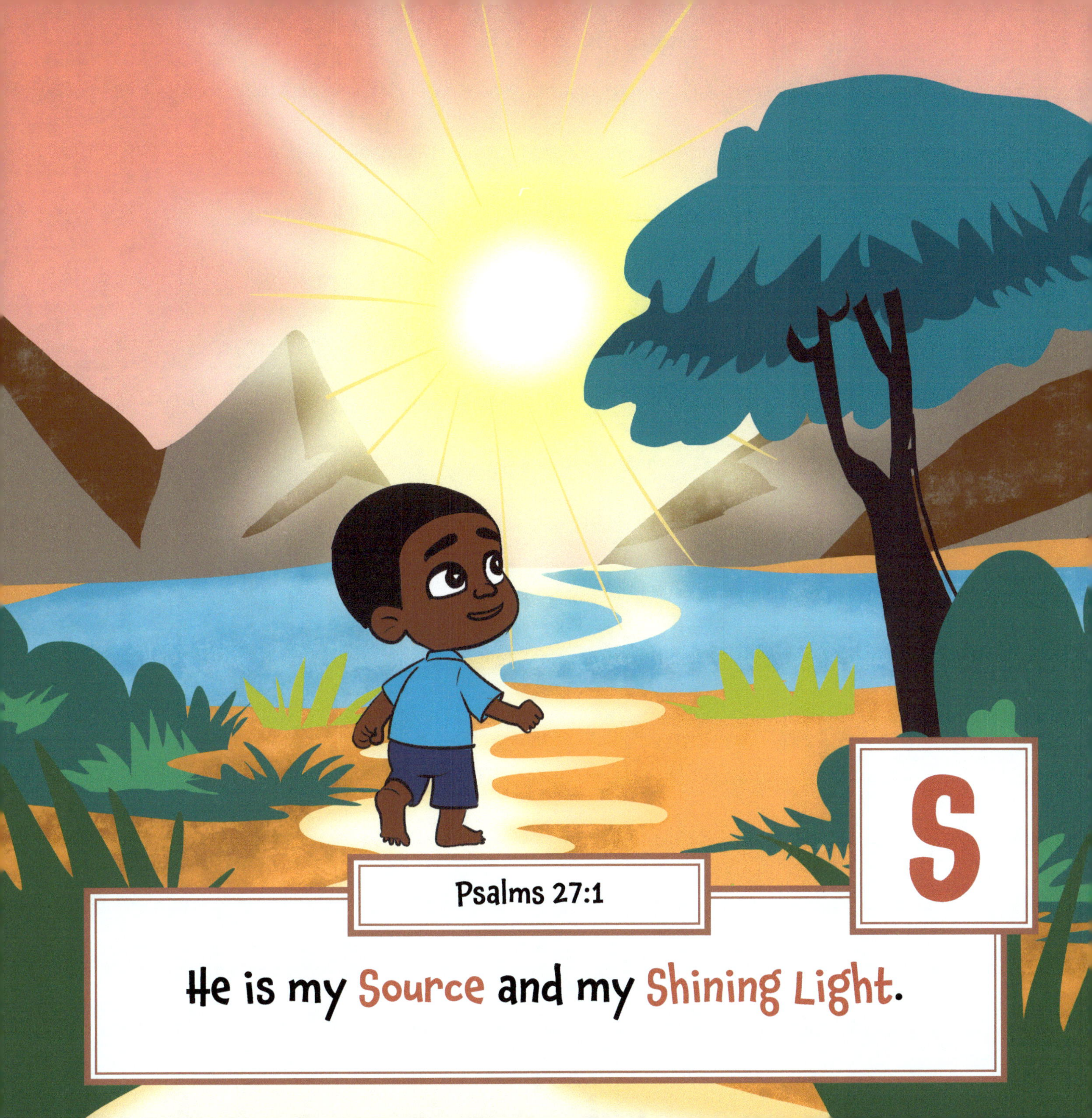
Psalms 27:1
S
He is my Source and my Shining Light.

T

Psalms 25:5

He is my Teacher.

Daniel 4:35
U
He is my Unquestionable God.

V
1 Corinthians 15:57
He is my Victorious God.

Jeremiah 33:6
He is my Wellbeing.
W

LOVE
†
X
Psalms 91
He is my Xtra Protection.

y
Exodus 6:2-3
He is my yahweh.

Z
Psalms 121:5
He is my Zion Keeper.

Acknowledgements

To the Almighty God, the source of all creativity and inspiration, who inspired and guided me as I wrote the pages of this book, I give my utmost gratitude. You are an all-encompassing God as seen in the pages of the book but most especially as you have shown and proven these characteristics of Yours to be true in my life. May this work be a testament to Your boundless love and Your true nature.

My deepest gratitude to my darling husband, Ebenezer Isaac whose wisdom is a true gift to me. Your kind support has been my bedrock. I appreciate your unending encouragement and your constant push for me to be better at my craft. I am endlessly thankful for your love and partnership!

To my dear children, Babajuwon and Oluwasewa, you are my greatest treasures and the source of inspiration. Your innocence, curiosity, and imagination have fueled my drive to write and finish the publication of this book – "Who is God to You?: The ABCs of Who God Is."

Thank you to my illustrator, Toluwanimi Babarinde for bringing to life my vision for the book.

Finally, to the readers—both young and young at heart—may the pages of this book ignite your imagination of who God is. I pray you get to know more and more about God through the pages of this amazing book.

With deepest gratitude and love,

Oyin Isaac

About the Author

Oyindamola "Oyin" Isaac

Oyindamola "Oyin" Isaac is an award-winning public speaker, author and certified human resources professional. She was honored in 2022 by the 100ABC Women as one of the 100 Accomplished Black Canadian Women and also recognized as one of Canada's Top 100 Black Women to Watch in 2023. Oyin was nominated for the Women of Inspiration Award and was awarded with the Rising Leader Award in 2024. Additionally, she received the 2024 Ontario Volunteer Service Award.

As an advocate for motherhood, she founded the non-profit A Sacred Motherhood Institute, dedicated to nurturing, empowering, and uplifting women from all walks of life. She is the author of "Motherhood, a Sacred Ministry." "Who is God to you?" is her debut children's book.

Oyin is also the creator of African Canadian Weddings, an online platform that celebrates and promotes event and wedding vendors within the African Canadian community. African Canadian Weddings has over 40,000 followers across Facebook (Meta) & Instagram.

Alongside her professional achievements, Oyin is a devoted mother and wife. She resides with her family in Mississauga, Ontario.